Index

A-10 Thunderbolt 9
Air Force Academy 21, 41
Bowman, Mark 36
Campbell, Kim 7, 8, 9, 10, 11, 16, 41, 42, 43, 44, 45
carrier landings 24
ejection 37, 38
Eurofighter Typhoon 33
F-16 32
F-22 17, 30
G-forces 26, 27, 33, 34
Gulf War 7, 14
Hampton, Dan 18, 25
heads-up display 34, 35
Hussein, Saddam 7
Iraq 7, 10, 43
Kuwait 11, 42
McGinn, Mike 14, 16
Naval Academy 21
pilot vocabulary 27
training 22, 23, 24, 28, 29
Turner, Richard 43
U.S. Air Force 7, 8, 15, 18, 19
U.S. Marines 7, 8, 10, 15
U.S. Navy 15
von Richthofen, Mandred 13
"Warthog" 9, 41
Wild Weasels 15
World War I 13
World War II 14

Photo Credits

Army Air Service: 12; Defence Imagery: 32; Department of Defense: 6; United States Air Force: Kenny Holston 6; Gertrude Zach 9; Jason Haag 10, 45; Cherie Thurlby 15; Raymond McCoy 20; 22; Samuel Rogers 25; Lee O. Tucker 30; Megan Floyd 35; Jonathan Snyder 38; Aaron Allman 40. United States Marine Corps/Preston Reed: 36. Newscom/UPI/Tanjufoto 42.

About the Author

Diane Bailey has written nearly forty nonfiction books for kids and teens, on topics ranging from science to sports to celebrities. She is particularly interested in learning how breakthroughs in science and technology are continually changing how people live. Diane also works as a freelance editor, usually from a chair in her living room in Kansas. She has two sons and two dogs, who are occasionally helpful in her work.

Series Glossary of Key Terms

apprehending capturing and arresting someone who has committed a crime

assassinate kill somebody, especially a political figure

assessment the act of gathering information and making a decision about a particular topic

contraband material that is illegal to possess

cryptography another word for writing in code

deployed put to use, usually in a military or law-enforcement operation

dispatcher a person who announces emergencies over police radio and helps organize the efforts of first responders

elite among the very best; part of a select group of successful experts

evacuated moved to a safe location, away from danger

federal related to the government of the United States, as opposed to the government of an individual state or city

forensic having to do with crime scene evidence

instinctive based on natural impulse and done without instruction

interrogate to question a person as part of an official investigation

Kevlar an extra-tough fabric used in bulletproof vests

search-and-rescue the work of finding survivors after a disaster occurs, or the team that does this work

stabilize make steady or secure; also, in medicine, make a person safe to transport

surveillance the act of watching another person or a place, usually from a hidden location

trauma any physical injury to the body, usually involving bleeding

visa travel permit issued by a government to a citizen for a specific trip

warrant official document that allows the police to do something, such as arrest a person

Find Out More

Books

Graham, Ian. *You Wouldn't Want to be a World War II Pilot!: Air Battles You Might Not Survive*. New York: Franklin Watts, 2010.

Parks, Peggy. *Fighter Pilot*. Farmington Hills, Mich.: Kidhaven, 2005.

Vansant, Wayne. *The Red Baron: The Graphic History of Richtofen's Flying Circus and the Air War in WWI*. Minneapolis: Zenith Press, 2014.

West, David. *Fighter Pilots*. New York: Rosen, 2008.

Web Sites

www.shmoop.com/careers/fighter-pilot/
This site gives a great introduction to what's involved with being a fighter pilot.

f15eeagle.tripod.com/manu.html
Check out some of the aerial maneuvers pilots learn here.

www.airforce.com/careers/detail/pilot/
People interested in a career with the Air Force can learn some basic information at this site.

www.navy.com/careers/aviation/naval-aviators.html#ft-key-responsibilities
If you are more interested in the Navy, check out this site for general information.

Campbell climbed out, uninjured, and was ready to fly again the next morning. That day's mission was to look for a pilot who had ejected after being shot down over Baghdad.

"Absolutely, I was going to go in there and do everything I could to pick him up," she said, "because that could have been me the day before."

Campbell earned a medal, the Distinguished Flying Cross, for her actions. However, it was the appreciation that she got from the Marines she helped in Baghdad that meant even more. Later that week, Campbell found a note left for her, scribbled on a napkin. It read, "If it hadn't been for you guys, I wouldn't still be here."

The path to the sky can be long and hard, but for those who have "the right stuff" to be a fighter pilot, it is those kinds of simple rewards that make it all worth it.

Safe on the ground, Campbell checked out the damage to her Warthog.

Campbell had a tough job in front of her, and she was anxious. Still, even with the huge challenges she faced, she felt confident she could do what she needed to. She knew her plane inside and out and believed it was one of the most reliable aircraft around. Her experience had prepared her to stay calm and cope with an emergency. She knew what to do; now she just had to do it.

"I had no doubt in my mind that I was going to land that airplane," she said.

The hour-long trip to travel through Iraq and into Kuwait felt like one of the longest of her life, but "when all three wheels hit the ground, it was an amazing feeling of relief," she said.

The relief was not only for her. Fellow soldiers and airmen on the ground were holding their breath as she steered her battered airplane toward the ground. Then she made a perfect landing in a crippled plane. The people watching were astonished by how well she handled it. Turner reported, "She landed in manual more smoothly than I landed with hydraulics."

rounding the cockpit was riddled with bullet holes, and the tail was severely damaged. Parts of the engine were breaking apart, with pieces of it being whisked away into the skies over Baghdad.

Campbell had two options: eject over enemy territory, or try to fly her crippled aircraft.

"If I have to pull these ejection handles… and I land in the middle of the [enemy]…this may not go so well for me," Campbell recalled.

In her two-ship formation, Campbell was the wingman. Beside her was Lt. Colonel Richard Turner. Right now, his job was to stick with Campbell. He was the more experienced pilot, but he could not make the decision for her. It was her call, and hers alone.

Campbell thought fast. Her training had prepared her to assess the situation—pros and cons—and then choose the best course of action.

Fortunately, even though her Warthog was severely damaged, it was still airborne—barely—amid the anti-aircraft fire. It was flying. Campbell decided to keep going.

Campbell faced anti-aircraft fire during her flight, similar to this action in a photo taken from later in the conflict.

the success rate was not encouraging. One time, the plane crashed and the pilot was killed. Another time, the plane split apart and caught fire, although the pilot was saved by a ground crew that pulled him from the wreckage in time. To even try to land the plane, Campbell had to make it to friendly territory in Kuwait, 300 miles away, and it was not clear if the Warthog would stay together that long. The "bathtub" of titanium armor sur-

Mission Accomplished!

Kim Campbell's plane was in a nose-dive over Baghdad. She'd been hit by a surface-to-air missile (SAM), and her A-10 Thunderbolt was severely damaged. The "Warthog" was designed with sophisticated systems that automatically control many aspects of flying the plane, but the SAM had knocked out that power. With those critical systems destroyed, Campbell had to go to a backup method called **manual reversion**. When all else has failed, that bare-bones method allows the pilot to use cranks and cables to execute the difficult maneuvers of flying. It's unbelievably difficult—and even more dangerous.

Flying her plane that way was hard enough, but Campbell knew that landing it was going to be even worse. The odds were stacked against her. Manual landings had been tried only a handful of times, and

Words to Understand

manual reversion a way of flying a plane without any automatic power or systems; the plane reverts, or switches back, to a state in which the pilot can operate it by hand, with his or her own power

Chapter 4

Captain Campbell was flying a Warthog like this one when she came through for her fellow soldiers in Iraq

code name. "I'm alive, and I need help." O'Grady was stranded for six days in enemy territory as rescuers frantically searched for him, but he didn't give up. Eventually, his radio signals directed his rescuers to within a few dozen yards of where he was hidden.

The right tools are only useful in the hands of people who have had the right training. Fighter pilots make sure they have both!

Text-Dependent Questions

1. Why do pilots use heads-up displays (HUDs)?
2. How does a G-suit work?
3. Name three things that a pilot might carry in a survival pack.

Research Project

What would you do if you were stranded? Make a list of what you think the bare essentials would be to keep you alive on the ground. What skills would you want to have?

Add to those skills the equipment pilots carry. Ejection seats have rafts built into them in case the pilot lands in water. The vest in his flight suit is also loaded with survival tools, including basic items such as matches, flares, a **tourniquet**, a whistle, and a compass. Special paint will **camouflage** his face in case he needs to hide. There are also global positioning system (GPS) devices and a radio to help rescuers find him.

In 1995, Air Force pilot Scott O'Grady's F-16 was hit by a surface-to-air missile while he was flying over Bosnia. The plane began to fall apart. The only way it was landing was in pieces—and O'Grady was determined not to be among those pieces. He ejected. Once he landed, he began sending messages. "This is Basher-52," he radioed, using his

Pilots do their work in the air, but they also must train for survival on the ground in case of an accident.

in the glasses. That helps pilots spot enemy targets and landing spots even when it's pitch-black!

Eject and Survive

Pilots do everything they can to land a plane, but if it is severely damaged, sometimes there is no other option but to eject. The pilot is already strapped into a special ejection seat. If his plane is going to crash, he can pull a lever that shoots him out of the plane. Then, a parachute carries him at a safe speed to the ground. Ejection, of course, can be dangerous in itself, but, fortunately, pilots who have ejected have a fairly good survival rate.

Once the pilots reach the ground, that's when the *real* survival begins. They may find themselves in a remote, desolate area, or in enemy territory. Fortunately, pilots have taken a survival program. In that course, they learn how to hunt and find other food, purify water, make tools and shelters, and navigate either in the daytime or at night. They also learn to how to signal for help, or, if necessary, to stay hidden.

Dressed in his flight suit, complete with paperwork tucked into a leg strap, a pilot inspects every inch of his airplane before climbing in.

so that the helmet knows which way the pilot is looking at any given moment. That way, the pilot can get information even if he is not looking straight ahead. Mark Bowman, a British test pilot who worked on designing new helmets, said, "We've moved away from the helmet being a crash helmet and a walkie-talkie into it being a sensor."

Wars do not only happen during the daytime so pilots have to be well-equipped to fly at night, as well. Although their jets are equipped with lights, the pilots often turn them off to reduce the risk of being seen. When the sun goes down, they get out their night-vision goggles. Those special glasses cost several thousand dollars, but they can pick up the slightest amount of light and make it glow green that is directly in the pilot's line of vision. He can get the information he needs and still see out the window.

Some HUDs are built directly into the pilot's helmet. The helmets have sensors on the outside. Cameras in the cockpit pick up information from the sensors and pass it onto computers,

When connected to the onboard computer, the pilot on the left will see information projected on his helmet-mounted heads-up display.

Attached to the top of the flight suit is the pilot's helmet. It's custom-made to fit the pilot's head and will help soften the blow if he hits his head. In addition, it helps reduce the pressure caused by G-force, which can cause headaches even at lower speeds. A hose connects the pilot's face to an oxygen supply. A tinted visor helps block the sun, and, since pilots need both hands for flying, a radio built into the helmet allows hands-free talking. Helmets also reduce the amount of external noise because fighter jets are loud machines!

Look Around

It can be distracting and dangerous for a pilot to look down at the instrument panel to check speed, altitude, or position. That's why the inside of the cockpit has a "heads-up display," or HUD. The HUD projects data onto a transparent screen

Nature Calls

Fighter pilots may spend many hours in the cockpit without a break. When nature calls, there is no convenient restroom. Some pilots carry "piddle packs." These bags are packed with a gel-like material that absorbs liquid. They can be clamped shut when full. Piddle packs have some problems, though. The pilot still has to squirm out of his flight suit—while flying—to use it, and sometimes they leak. Another solution is a special system worn inside the flight suit that drains urine into an external bag. There's one version for men and another for women.

Getting Dressed

During periods of extreme acceleration, G-force causes blood to pool up in the legs and feet of a pilot. If not enough blood gets to the brain, the pilot can pass out. To withstand the intense pressure of G-force, pilots wear a special suit called the G-suit. The jumpsuit is filled with air that circulates around the body and squeezes the lower torso and legs to force blood back up to the heart and brain.

Underneath a G-suit, pilots may wear an exposure suit, which is similar to a wet suit worn by divers. If pilots get stranded in cold weather, or have to eject into chilly water, the exposure suit will help hold in their body heat. Some modern exposure suits provide a measure of protection against other dangers, such as biological or chemical weapons.

Tomorrow's Cockpit

It can take decades to design and manufacture a fighter jet. Some of the jets being flown today were first thought of back in the 1970s. Today's designers must think ahead to what pilots will need in 30 or 40 years. Test pilot Mark Bowman has helped in the design of the Eurofighter Typhoon, a fighter jet used in the British Royal Air Force. Over the last few decades, the design of planes has improved greatly, making the actual business of flying the airplane easier on pilots. Now, he says, "The role of the pilot moves more into mission management. It's about decision-making." Future cockpit technologies could help pilots with strategic tasks, such as tracking other aircraft or watching troops on the ground.

Super-hot flames burst from the rear exhaust ports of a fighter jet as it prepares to reach the speed needed for takeoff.

the plane a burst of power. With that extra thrust from its afterburners, it can be 20,000 feet (6 km) high in less than a minute.

Fighter jets have extraordinary maneuverability. They are made to fly in all kinds of positions—on their sides, upside-down—and turn quickly and sharply. That means that if they are attacking an enemy on the ground, they can make several passes within only a few seconds.

It's just as important to be able to escape. In these jets, fighter pilots can dip, dive, and roll to evade an enemy jet or anti-aircraft weapons. The F-16 is one jet used in the Air Force. It's a very maneuverable plane and is designed to be good at attacking either air or ground targets. "[With] the F-16 and the role that we perform today, the airplane is the difference," says Major Ray "Hollywood" Fowler, an F-16 flight lead. "We own the sky."

Tools and Technology

The cockpits of fighter jets are small, but they've got just enough room for the pilot—and the forty pounds of gear he or she carries. Fighter pilots fly multi-million-dollar machines, put their lives at risk, and work to save others. Every piece of equipment they have is designed to help their odds of success.

The Planes

The airplane nicknames say it all: Hornet, Strike Eagle, Falcon, Raptor. The feathered natural **predators** of the sky are powerful and dangerous, and so are military fighter jets named for them. The airships fly high and fast, reaching altitudes and speeds that make a commercial airliner seem tame. A commercial jet might cruise at 30,000 feet and 550 miles per hour. A fighter jet, on the other hand, might fly twice that high and more than three times as fast. Fighter jets are equipped with **afterburners**, which inject additional fuel into the engine to give the plane a burst

Words to Understand

afterburners part of an engine that injects extra fuel into the engine to provide more thrust
camouflage to disguise something by making it blend into its surroundings
predators hunters; animals that feed on more vulnerable animals
tourniquet a bandage that reduces or cuts off the flow of blood to a limb

Chapter 3

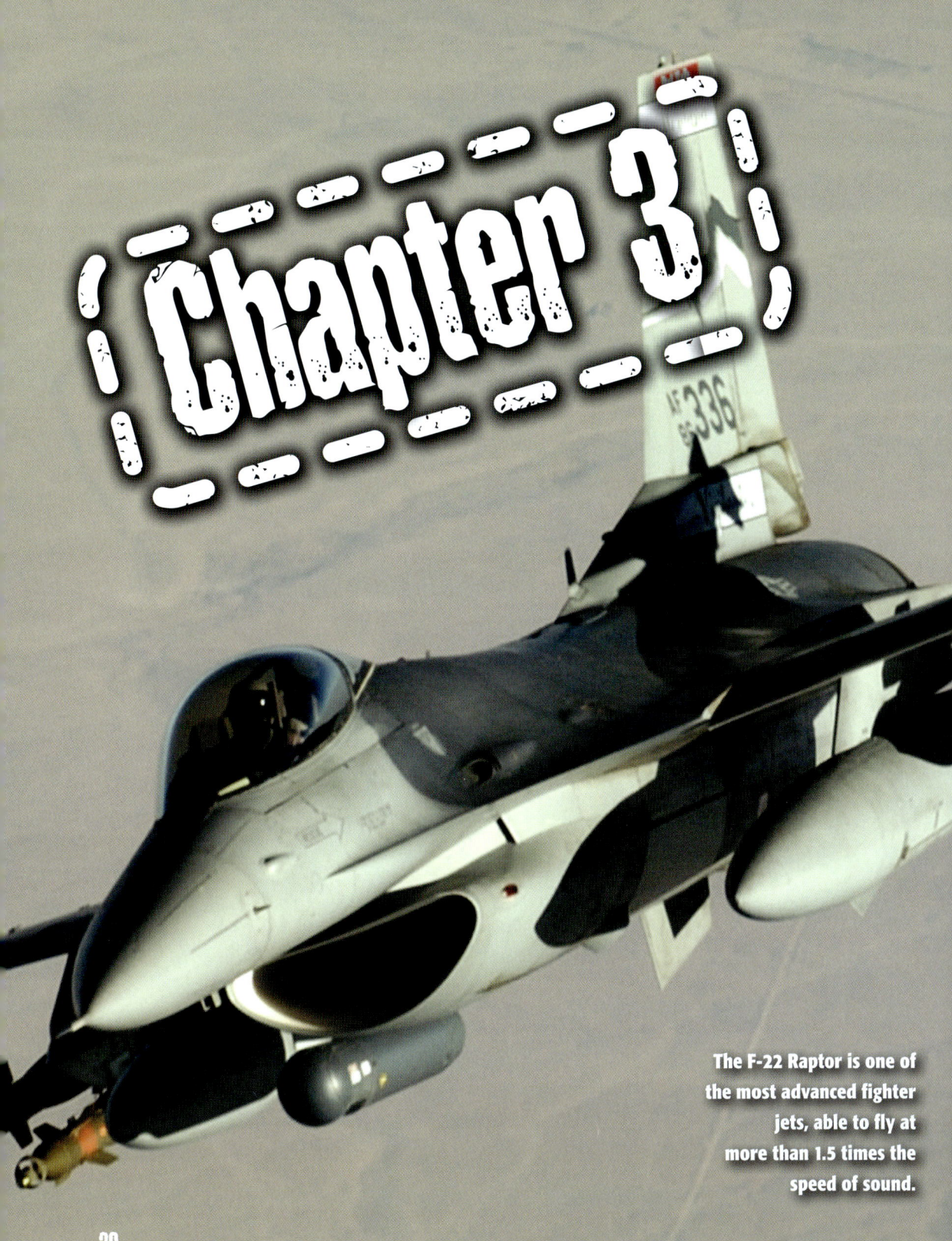

The F-22 Raptor is one of the most advanced fighter jets, able to fly at more than 1.5 times the speed of sound.

pilot will escort the aircraft out of the no-fly zone. If it's a deliberate intrusion, the pilot could be called upon to use the jet's weapons.

It takes approximately two years for pilots to finish all the required training. In return, they are expected to make a commitment to the military. The military invests a lot of time and money into training pilots, so they must serve for several years. Once all the training is completed, however, a pilot finally hears the words he's been waiting for: He is "mission ready."

Text-Dependent Questions

1. What are three requirements for becoming a pilot?
2. Why is too much G-force dangerous for a person?
3. What are some duties that pilots might have in addition to flying?

Research Project

Fighter pilots learn a variety of complex aerial maneuvers. Do some research to find out more about barrel rolls, yo-yos, spirals, and more. Describe how they work.

Ups and Downs

All of a fighter pilot's training is designed to get him or her ready for a day at work—but there's no typical "day in a life" in this job. Missions can start in the middle of the afternoon or the middle of the night. They might last a couple of hours, and during wartime, pilots may have to do several missions in a row, without a break. That means they could spend eight or ten hours strapped into their seat before they land. Pilots typically also have another job besides flying. They might help with scheduling, train other pilots, or handle weapons. A pilot's day often runs 12 hours or even more.

More fighter pilots are needed during times of active war, but they still have jobs to do in peacetime. The borders of the United States are constantly guarded. So are certain areas within the country, such as the White House, the Pentagon, and the Capitol Building in Washington, D.C. If an aircraft flies there without permission, a fighter jet may be sent to intercept the intruder and find out what's going on. If it's simply a mistake, the fighter

person's skin out of place, as if a powerful wind is blowing it backward, but it's inside the body the bigger changes happen. The G-force pulls blood away from the brain, which can cause major problems. A pilot may temporarily lose his vision, and if too much blood floods away from the brain, he could pass out.

Pilots practice how to counteract G-force by spending time in a **centrifuge**. A centrifuge is like a high-powered merry-go-round. Imagine sitting in a cab at the very edge of the merry-go-round, connected to the central pole by a long arm or tube. In a centrifuge, the trainee sits in the cab and is spun at high speeds to simulate G-force. "It feels like weight is pushing down on every part of you," says pilot Jack Stewart. Pilots can regulate their breathing by pushing air out of their lungs, and flex the muscles in their shoulders and legs to keep blood flowing upward toward the brain.

Talk the Talk

Fighter pilots have their own way of saying things. The words can be confusing to civilians, but they make sense if you know the code. Here are a few examples:

- **check six**—look behind you, at the position of "6" on a clock
- **lights out**—flying without radar
- **punch out**—eject
- **scramble jets**—get the aircraft ready to fly in a hurry
- **shiny side**—the top of the airplane (the bottom is the "greasy" side)

Put the Pressure On

The sky is not a friendly place. At high altitudes, there is limited oxygen in the air, and the temperatures are extremely cold. The pilot is protected in the cockpit, but just in case, he wears a cozy flight suit and an oxygen mask at all times.

The speeds at which a pilot travels pose another challenge. Some fighter jets can fly at 1,800 miles (2,986 km) per hour. That's about three times the speed of sound! Such speeds produce a great physical pressure on the pilot, called G-force. G stands for gravity. Gravity produces pressure anywhere, and people are used to it under normal conditions on the ground. A person standing on the ground is experiencing 1 G. A person riding a roller coaster might briefly experience 5 or 6 Gs when hurtling down. The body can withstand some increases in G-force for a couple of seconds.

A fighter pilot may experience 8 or 9 Gs for several seconds, and slightly lower force for 20 or 30 seconds. Those kinds of numbers put extreme stress on the body. Extreme G-force can push a

and the fuel tanker line up one above the other. A hose connects the two planes, and fuel flows from one to the other. Because the two planes are connected, it's vital to keep the same speed and position, so it is precision flying at its best. Retired Air Force pilot Dan Hampton writes in his book *Viper Pilot*, "Think of your wet tongue stuck to a frozen pipe being towed behind a car at three hundred miles per hour, and you get the idea."

A midair refueling calls for a high-speed dance thousands of feet in the air. The pilots must be in perfect formation.

Carrier Landings

Navy pilots are specially trained to land on aircraft carriers. These ships provide a base for planes in the middle of the sea. They are only about 1,000 feet long, so the planes must stop fast! Cables attached to the ship hook onto the plane to stop it within about 300 feet. If the plane misses the cables, it must take off again—before the runway ends—and circle around to re-try.

Any pilot must learn the basics of how to operate a plane. Fighter pilots take it a step farther. Their jets are designed to fly upside-down or on their sides, to rise fast—and drop faster. Pilots learn several specialized maneuvers that take advantage of those capabilities. They're not doing those stomach-dropping acrobatics for fun. The moves help them get the best strategic position in a fight. For example, in a barrel roll, the plane rolls over as it turns. In a yo-yo, pilots either dive down or pull upward. In a dive, the plane gains speed to chase after a target, while pulling up gives the aircraft more altitude and can help it match the speed of a target.

Perhaps one of the most important "moves" is getting fuel. Fighter jets are extraordinary gas guzzlers. Sometimes pilots are in the middle of a mission and don't have time to land and refuel. In such cases, there's a gas station in the sky: another aircraft. In a midair refueling, the fighter jet

to pass. American pilots must be U.S. citizens and pass a background check that will ensure they get security clearance.

Next, it's on to get a physical screening. Future fighter pilots must be of average height and weight, with good vision and hearing. They must be in good enough shape to endure intense physical training. Push-ups, sit-ups, and timed runs are all part of the qualifications. Finally, they take a turn in a **flight simulator.** This introduces them to the basics of flight, and evaluates whether they will be able to learn and excel at the skills needed to fly. After that, the more specialized training begins.

All the Right Moves

Much of the pilots' training takes place in the classroom. There, they learn management skills, military history, and war strategies. They also study the math and science behind flying, called **aeronautics**. It's important to understand the physics of flight to operate a plane effectively. However, it's when they get in the cockpit that the real fun begins.

Candidates must pass a series of academic and ability tests. They include subjects such as math, general science, verbal skills, and the ability to read and understand instruments used in flying. In the Air Force, candidates take a five-hour test with almost 400 questions! They get two chances

In a flight simulator, a trainee reacts to video shown all around him as he learns to guide his aircraft.

Training Mind and Body

Fighter pilots work under enormous stress. Other people's lives depend on them, and they risk death on a regular basis. When there are split-second decisions to be made, they do not have time to check the manual to see what to do. Performing well in such circumstances is part instinct, but a lot of it comes from good training.

Becoming a Pilot

Getting a college degree and becoming a military officer are the first steps in a fighter pilot's journey. Many trainees go to the Air Force Academy or Naval Academy to do that. Another route is to graduate from a civilian college and then attend a special school to become an officer.

Words to Understand

aeronautics the principles and science involved with flying
centrifuge a machine that spins at high speeds to create force
flight simulator a stationary machine that imitates what it is like to fly; it is used to train pilots

Chapter 2

Reading while they march, students aiming for the Air Force Academy and a career as a pilot start at the Academy Prep School.

It's helpful to understand the math and science of flying when you're in the air moving at high speeds.

It takes years of training to become a fighter pilot, and many candidates wash out before they make it. For those who succeed, however, the rewards can be huge. Mark Lavardiere served twenty years with the U.S. Air Force and wrote a book called *A Fighter Pilot's Story*. In it, he writes, "There is no better office space in the world than in the cockpit of a fighter jet!"

Text-Dependent Questions

1. What is the name for a backup pilot in a formation?
2. What was the job of the Wild Weasels?
3. Name a type of job that is good for RPAs, or drones.

Research Project

Before being accepted into a military program, candidates go through an interview to see if they will be a good fit. Consider your answers to the following questions: Why do you want to be a pilot? What do you know about how military pilots work? What sort of lifestyle do you want to lead? How would being a fighter pilot work into your plans for the future?

The Right Stuff

The image of fighter pilots is one of people who are brave and tough. It is important to remember, however, that their confidence is blended with shrewd decision-making. They consider all the options and circumstances, but they are ready to act fast when they have to—sometimes within fractions of seconds. Dan Hampton, a retired Air Force pilot, says, "Fighter pilots, by nature, can function well when everything around them is falling apart."

Physical fitness and stamina are key to being a good fighter pilot. Fighter pilots fly at high altitudes, and at speeds that break the sound barrier. Flying that fast is very hard on the human body. Add to that being stuffed into a tiny cockpit, with enemy fire coming from below, and the stress levels go up.

Nerves of steel and a body of iron aren't the only qualifications. Fighter pilots have to be smart. They're required to be college graduates. Although they can study anything they want, most choose degrees that focus on math or on science.

being used more often by the military. No one flies inside the aircraft itself, so drones do not put a pilot at risk. Drones are good at tasks such as conducting surveillance and attacking ground targets.

"We're at the point where RPA pilots are getting the most combat experience of anyone," says one Air Force pilot.

"The important thing for me is the twenty-year-old with the rifle on the ground, sleeping in a ditch. That's why we do this job. Would I like to be flying an F-22 around and doing loops and rolls and things? Sure, absolutely. But I find what I do now to be more meaningful than anything else I could think of."

Drones will probably not replace human pilots altogether, however. Pilots on the scene process all kinds of information almost instantly. They can read their instruments, but also can see, hear, and sense in the moment. That's difficult for any drone, no matter how advanced, to do as well as a human.

Saving Lives

Marines were on the ground in Afghanistan as the call came in from the aircraft controller: "Our guys are getting shot up," came the report. They needed immediate air support. If they did not get it, the outcome was grim: "Americans are gonna die." Air Force pilots Mike McGinn and Ray Fowler zoomed to the scene. "We heard the words, 'Danger Close,' meaning we are going to be [arriving] right in the middle of their fight," said Fowler. To make the situation more complicated, the fight was in the middle of a town, and the pilots were worried about their weapons hitting the wrong targets—friendly forces or innocent **civilians**. Tense moments passed as the pilots waited for a clear shot, but finally they got it. The ground troops were relieved—and so were the pilots. "What we did that day saved American lives," said McGinn.

flight lead. The backup is the wingman. (They can also fly in larger groups.)

The job has historically attracted men. Since 1993, women have been allowed to be fighter and bomber pilots in the U.S. military, although their numbers are still far lower than men. When pilot Kim Campbell flew her nail-biting mission in 2003, she was one of about 50 female fighter pilots in the Air Force. "The important thing is to work really hard and be good at it, and then nobody cares what gender you are," she said. "I'm not a female fighter pilot. I'm just a fighter pilot, and I love it."

Drones

Some fighter pilots don't even take to the skies. Instead, they head to work inside an office. With a computer and joystick, they fly remotely piloted aircraft (RPAs), also called **drones**. Drones are

not directed at another, more vulnerable, target. One group of Air Force pilots was called the "Wild Weasels." Their job was not to avoid enemy fire, but to encourage it. As enemy forces fired surface-to-air missiles, the Weasels were able to protect other targets as well as identify where enemies—and their weapons—were hidden.

The mission of a Wild Weasel squadron is to attract enemy fire—but it is also well equipped to dish out a little firepower of its own.

In the United States, the Air Force, the Navy, and the Marines employ fighter pilots. (They are called "naval aviators" in the Navy because in that service, the word "pilot" describes the operator of a ship.) The Air Force has a much larger force of aircraft and pilots, but any branch might be called on for air support—it just depends who is closer to the action. Pilots typically fly in teams, often of two or four. The planes are called "ships." In a two-ship formation, the most experienced pilot is the

Since then, fighter pilots have played an important role in major conflicts, from World War II in the 1940s to the Gulf Wars in the 1990s and 2000s. "Every fighter pilot remembers the first time they deployed in combat and how special that moment was," says Air Force Lt. Col. Mike "Homie" McGinn. "Fighter pilot is not just a job. It's an attitude; it's a mentality."

In the Cockpit

Dogfights such as those fought during the World Wars are less common among today's fighter pilots. Occasionally, pilots must engage in direct air-to-air combat, firing their weapons at each other while executing aerial maneuvers. Most of the time, however, fighter pilots are called on for other kinds of missions. They make attacks called **sorties**. They may shoot at enemy soldiers to protect friendly forces on the ground. They may also try to destroy the enemy's weapons and supplies. Some pilots try to distract or confuse the enemy, or purposely try to draw enemy fire so that it is

Mission Prep

Barely one hundred years ago, the job of fighter pilot did not even exist. Airplanes themselves were cutting-edge technology. World War I began in 1914, and the first military planes were used to drop bombs and to act as scouts, collecting information about what was happening. Soon, engineers found ways to arm planes with other weapons that could be used in direct combat.

By the end of World War I, fighter pilots routinely engaged in **dogfights**—battles between planes in air-to-air combat. For such battles, the airmen became fighter pilots. Probably the most famous fighter pilot of all time was Manfred von Richthofen, a German pilot who was nicknamed the "Red Baron" because of his red airplane. He chalked up some eighty victories before being shot down near the end of the war.

Words to Understand

civilians non-military personnel; regular people
dogfights battles between planes that take place entirely in the air
drones aircraft that carry no pilot on board and are controlled remotely
sorties attacks made from a defensive position

Chapter 1

World War I pilots flew lightweight biplanes. The wings were made of fabric stretched over wood and metal.

plane. Without a working hydraulics system, Campbell had no steering, no brakes, no ability to land . . . not unless she could fly the plane manually. It was her only option, so she switched over to that backup method.

Now she had another choice to make. One option was to try to fly the plane, or what was left of it. She had some 300 miles (482 km) to cover before she would reach Kuwait and friendly airspace.

Her other option was to eject over Baghdad. She would shoot herself out of the plane, leaving it to crash. That would ruin the plane and possibly injure innocent people on the ground. In addition, Campbell would be ejecting into enemy territory. She'd just been shooting at them, and they'd just been shooting at her. So, back to Option One.

Later, in the final "Mission Accomplished" chapter, see how Captain Campbell found the solution to her problem. First, read more about the steps pilots take to reach their goals in the sky.

This view of the rear of Campbell's airplane shows some of the damage from the enemy ground force's weapons.

As Campbell looked to the ground, she saw the Iraqis only a quarter of a mile away from the Marines, and closing in. She had to close in faster. Every second counted. Flying through a dust storm at 200 miles per hour, she assessed the situation, identifying the friendly forces from the enemy. Then she aimed her powerful cannon, and let loose.

Campbell's attack reached her target, but it also drew attention to her. The Iraqis fought back, firing at Campbell's plane. The armor on her plane clanged as a barrage of bullets found their marks. Suddenly, Campbell heard an explosion, and her plane bucked out of control. She'd been hit! A surface-to-air missile (SAM) had found its mark. Her 15-ton aircraft veered violently to the left and began a nose-dive toward the city below.

Caution lights lit up on the control panel as the plane suffered one failure after another. The worst one was the **hydraulics** system, which provided power to many critical systems on the

recognize the situation the guys on the ground are in . . . and you do what you can, as quickly as you can, to help the guys on the ground," Campbell remembered later.

Campbell's plane was also designed specifically for close-air support. She was flying an A-10 Thunderbolt. Its nickname in the Air Force is a "Warthog." An actual warthog is not very attractive or graceful, and neither is the plane. In fact, it's kind of an ugly thing. Even though it is not as sleek or fast as some of the military's other fighter jets, that's not the point. The Warthog is designed to fly low and slow, so it can get in close to the target and have enough time to fire. It's a tough, durable plane, constructed like a flying tank. Titanium armor protects the outside, and it's loaded with powerful weapons.

Campbell's A-10 Thunderbolt features wing-mounted cannons along with air-to-ground missiles.

the Marines advanced, the Iraqis began hurling **grenades** and peppering the Marines with machine-gun fire. The Marines fought back, but the Iraqis were well protected and heavily armed. Stuck on an open bridge, the Marines were easy targets. They realized there was no getting across the bridge without suffering heavy **casualties** . . . not without help, anyway.

That's where Campbell came in. The Air Force captain was on her way to another site, but then her radio crackled with a call. The Marines were requesting close-air support, meaning they needed aircraft to swoop in at close range—maybe at an altitude of only a few hundred feet—and fire on the enemy.

Fortunately, close-air support was Campbell's specialty, and she knew what she was doing. Even though she was only 27 years old, she'd been in combat before. Her initials were K.C., and her fellow pilots had given her the **call sign** "Killer Chick." Knowing that Marines below her were in danger, she raced to help the trapped soldiers. "You

U.S. Air Force fighter pilot Kim Campbell flew thousands of feet over Baghdad. Below her, the Iraqi city was at war. It was a mess of shattered windows and abandoned buildings. The streets were littered with rubble from all the shooting and bombing. It was April 2003, during the second Gulf War. As Campbell flew overhead, American troops were locked in a fierce battle with the Republican Guard, a dedicated—and deadly—branch of the Iraqi army.

The goal of the American forces was to take over the city of Baghdad and overthrow the country's leader, the **dictator** Saddam Hussein. To do that, they had to control a few important places within the city, cutting off the flow of people and supplies that was supporting the Republican Guard. One of those places was a bridge over the Tigris River, in the northern part of the city.

A unit of Marines marched to the bridge, hoping to prevent Iraqi soldiers from entering the city. The Iraqis, though, had other ideas. As

Words to Understand

call sign the nickname given to a pilot by fellow pilots
casualties deaths and injuries caused by war
dictator an extremely powerful ruler who often mistreats his citizens
grenades small, short-range bombs that can be thrown by hand
hydraulics a way of using liquids to distribute force; this force can help power mechanical systems

Ground crew members prepare the airplanes before fighter pilots take to the air to complete their missions.

Emergency!

Contents

Emergency!	6
Mission Prep	12
Training Mind and Body	20
Tools and Technology	30
Mission Accomplished!	40
Find Out More	46
Series Glossary	47
Index/About the Author	48

Key Icons to Look For

Words to Understand: These words with their easy-to-understand definitions will increase the reader's understanding of the text, while building vocabulary skills.

Sidebars: This boxed material within the main text allows readers to build knowledge, gain insights, explore possibilities, and broaden their perspectives by weaving together additional information to provide realistic and holistic perspectives.

Research Projects: Readers are pointed toward areas of further inquiry connected to each chapter. Suggestions are provided for projects that encourage deeper research and analysis.

Text-Dependent Questions: These questions send the reader back to the text for more careful attention to the evidence presented here.

Series Glossary of Key Terms: This back-of-the-book glossary contains terminology used throughout this series. Words found here increase the reader's ability to read and comprehend higher-level books and articles in this field.

Mason Crest
450 Parkway Drive, Suite D
Broomall, PA 19008
www.masoncrest.com

© 2016 by Mason Crest, an imprint of National Highlights, Inc.
All rights reserved. No part of this publication may be reproduced or transmitted in any form or by any means, electronic or mechanical, including photocopying, recording, taping, or any information storage and retrieval system, without permission from the publisher.

Printed and bound in the United States of America.

Series ISBN: 978-1-4222-3391-7
Hardback ISBN: 978-1-4222-3395-5
EBook ISBN: 978-1-4222-8504-6

First printing
1 3 5 7 9 8 6 4 2

Produced by Shoreline Publishing Group LLC
Santa Barbara, California
Editorial Director: James Buckley Jr.
Designer: Bill Madrid
Production: Sandy Gordon
www.shorelinepublishing.com
Cover image: U.S. Air Force/Master Sgt. Lance Cheung

Library of Congress Cataloguing-in-Publication Data

Bailey, Diane, 1966-
  Fighter pilot / by Diane Bailey.
       pages cm. -- (On a mission!)
  Includes index.
   ISBN 978-1-4222-3395-5 (hardback : alk. paper) -- ISBN 978-1-4222-3391-7 (series : alk. paper) -- ISBN 978-1-4222-8504-6 (ebook) 1. Fighter pilots--United States. 2. Airplanes--Piloting. I. Title.   UG626.B35 2015
 358.4'302373--dc23
                                                            2015004836

ON A MISSION

Fighter Pilot

by Diane Bailey

ON A MISSION

Bomb Squad Technician

Border Security

Dogs on Patrol

FBI Agent

Fighter Pilot

Firefighter

Paramedic

Search and Rescue Team

Secret Service Agent

Special Forces

SWAT Team

Undercover Police Officer

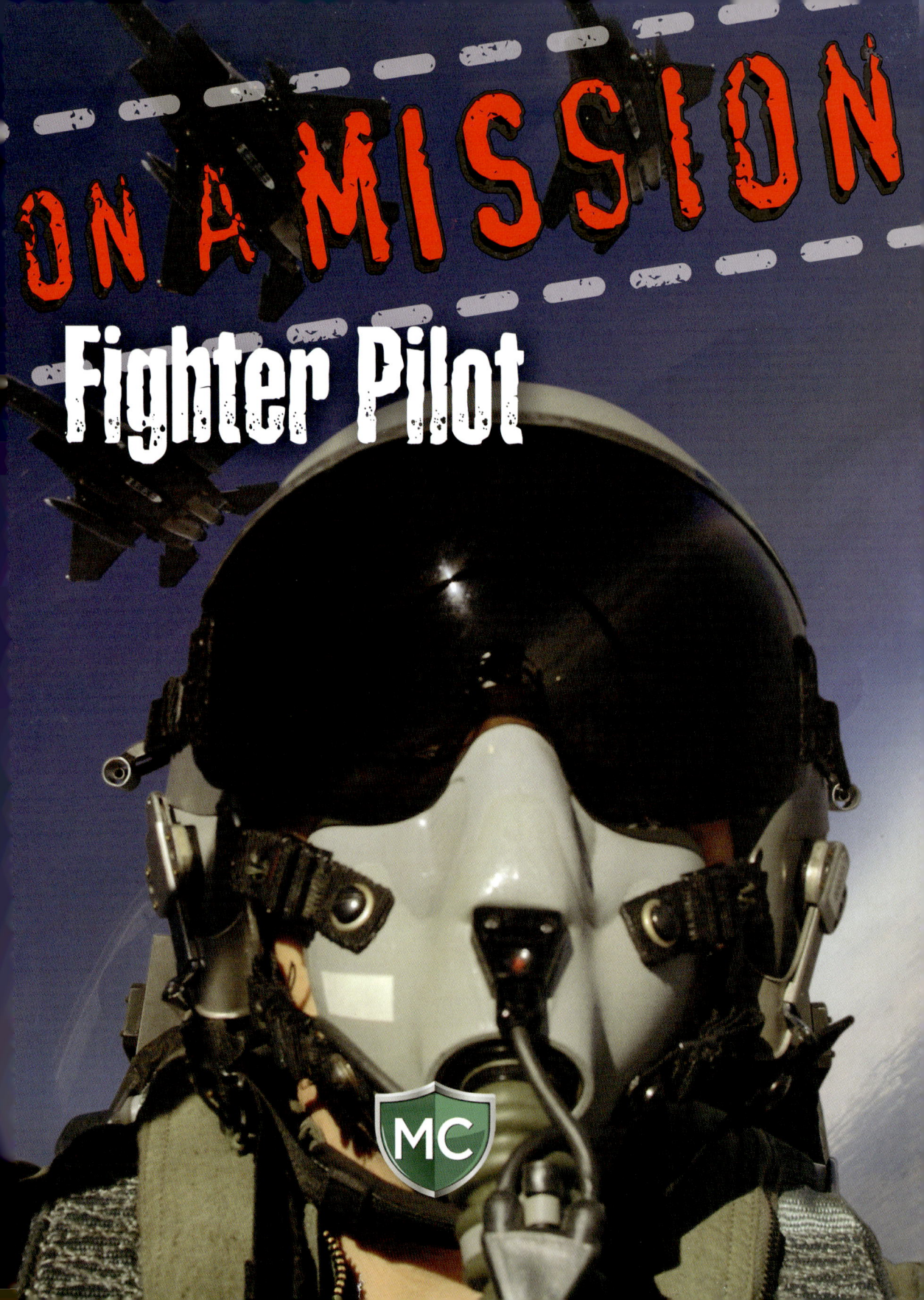